30 Fun Ways to Learn About Counting

by Clare Beswick

30 FUN WAYS to Learn About COUNTING

CLARE BESWICK
ILLUSTRATED BY K. WHELAN DERY

© 2011 Gryphon House, Inc.
Published by Gryphon House, Inc.
10770 Columbia Pike, Suite 201
Silver Spring, MD 20901
800.638.0928; 301.595.9500; 301.595.0051 (fax)

Visit us on the web at www.gryphonhouse.com

Originally published in 2009 by A&C Black Publishers Limited 36 Soho Square, London W1D 3QY
acblack.com, and in 2007 by Featherstone Education

Illustrations: K. Whelan Dery
Cover Art: © iStockphoto LP 2009. All rights reserved. iStockphoto® and iStock® are trademarks of
iStockphoto LP. Flash® is a registered trademark of Adobe Inc. www.istockphoto.com.
Many thanks to Turnbridge Day Nursery

Library of Congress Cataloging-in-Publication Data
Beswick, Clare.
  30 fun ways to learn about counting / Clare Beswick.
      p. cm.
  ISBN 978-0-87659-367-7
  1. Counting—Juvenile literature. I. Title. II. Title: Thirty fun ways to learn about counting.
  QA113.B475 2011
  513.2'11--dc22
                                      2010043562

Bulk purchase
Gryphon House books are available for special premiums and sales promotions as well as for
fund-raising use. Special editions or book excerpts also can be created to specification. For details,
contact the Director of Marketing at Gryphon House.

Disclaimer
Gryphon House, Inc. and the author cannot be held responsible for damage, mishap, or injury
incurred during the use of or because of activities in this book. Appropriate and reasonable caution
and adult supervision of children involved in activities and corresponding to the age and capability
of each child involved is recommended at all times. Do not leave children unattended at any time.
Observe safety and caution at all times.

Contents

Introduction 7

Activities

Bowling Pin Splash 14

Ping-Pong Fun 16

Spotted Dogs 18

Beat that Drum 20

Ten Terrible Dinosaurs 22

Big Box Guessing Game 24

Pirates' Treasure 26

Hip Hop, Bunny Hop 28

Traffic Jam 30

Mini Mosaics 32

Kangaroos Against the Clock 34

Knives, Forks, and Spoons 36

Gobble, Gobble, Munch, Crunch 38

One, Two, Three, Four, Five 40

Down the Drain 42

Ten in the Bed 44

Pasta Picnics 46

Bubble Fun 48

Circle Time Treasure 50

What's That? 52

S-t-r-e-t-c-h! 54

Perfume Making 56

Lemon and Lime Surprise 58

It's a Goal! 60

Tricky Triangles 62

Clip Art Crazy 64

Count Those Spots 66

Firefighters and Ladders 68

Hoops and Loops 70

Finger Fun 72

Index **74**

Introduction

Counting is a skill that we all use every day. It is such a fundamental part of our everyday lives that it is difficult to think back and analyze how we learned to understand basic number concepts.

Counting starts in the cradle. With even the tiniest babies, parents sing and play, clap two hands, tickle 10 toes, wiggle five fingers, and kiss one nose! The very foundations of our knowledge and counting skills start as soon as we are able to identify everyday objects and body parts. As babies and children discover patterns, sameness, and difference among objects, shapes, pictures, and patterns, they are able to form pairs and groups by sorting and sharing. To give meaning to these groups and divisions, we use number names to define quantity.

At first, children may learn the number names by imitation and use them in a random sequence. It takes time and practice to put these number names in order and give them some meaning, but gradually children begin to understand the idea of one-to-one correspondence, matching one object or action to one count, sharing objects, one for each child, and so on. At this stage, children need a lot of practice in as many different everyday situations as we can provide.

When children are able to match and sort objects and pictures, they can then begin to gain an understanding of counting groups and using number words to describe quantities, such as two shoes or six pens. At first, children will need to count the objects in the group one by one but, with practice and maturity, they will be able to glance at the group and identify the quantity visually. This skill starts with guessing and is refined into estimation. Guessing and estimating, then counting to check, provide great opportunities to gain confidence and have fun with counting. It also prompts the use of mathematical words and concepts, such as "few," "many," "lots," and "hundreds." Children also need to discover the concept of nothing or zero. This is a natural progression from all those very early play and gesture games of "All Gone."

Children then quickly discover more mathematical language and ideas, and are able to use these skills to make sense of everyday situations, to solve problems, to plan, to wonder what might happen, to estimate, and to predict. They can use their knowledge of numbers and counting to explore, make comparisons, formulate new ideas, and calculate.

As children continue to work with groups of objects, matching and sorting, they need to have opportunities to count combined groups of objects, to add one more, take one away, share between two children, and look at groups and pairs of objects. In this way, children begin to discover the twin concepts of finding the sum or total of two groups of objects and of subtraction: "How many will I have if I take some away?"

Sorting objects into pairs helps children learn counting by twos. Socks, shoes, and gloves are invaluable for this activity, as are hands and fingers for counting by fives! Take off socks and shoes, wiggle fingers and toes, and count by fives and 10s.

And don't forget children can and should learn to count using:

- Everyday objects, large and small;
- Experiences such as counting steps, stairs, and so on;
- Groups of the same objects and groups of mixed objects;
- Actions, action songs, and counting rhymes;
- Body parts;
- Sounds in the environment and those made with instruments and body parts;
- Moving and stationary objects;
- Pictures and line drawings;
- Photographs;
- Objects of different sizes and shapes;
- 2D and 3D shapes, symbols, and patterns;
- Objects they can touch and those they cannot;
- Images on a screen;
- Things that appear and disappear, such as bubbles, as well as objects that persist;
- Touch pointing, pointing, and eye pointing; and
- Techniques of counting forward and counting backward.

Children also need to record what they have counted in a variety of ways by:

- Drawing pictures or symbols;
- Drawing circles or dots;
- Tallying, for example, /// /// = 6;
- Placing counters or buttons;
- Using number labels or cards;
- Taking pictures;
- Using white boards, clipboards, flip charts, and chalkboards;
- Using hand tally counters; and
- Using chalk on the ground.

The wide range of simple, everyday activities in this book gives young children opportunities to use their emerging counting and math skills.

Using numbers as "labels" and for counting:

- Say and use number names in order in familiar contexts;
- Count reliably up to ten everyday objects;
- Recognize numerals one to 10; and
- Use developing mathematical ideas and methods to solve practical problems.

Calculating:

- In practical activities and discussion, begin to use the vocabulary involved in adding and subtracting;
- Use language such as "more" or "less" to compare two quantities;
- Find one more or one less than a number from one to 10; and
- Begin to relate addition to combining two groups of objects, and subtraction to taking away.

Understanding shape, space, and measures:

- Talk about, recognize, and recreate patterns; and
- Use developing mathematical ideas and methods to solve practical problems.

Essential Attention-Grabbing-and-Keeping Tips

The exaggerated gasp!

A sudden sharp intake of breath can work wonders.

Hold that pause!

Pausing at just the right moment and holding it for a few seconds longer than expected will leave the children eager to know what is coming next.

Listen!

Tilt your head to one side and reach towards your ear with a "What's that I hear?" gesture. Most children will stop and look at you to see what you can hear.

Do something different!

Sit somewhere unexpected, give a huge stretch, shake out your arms, wriggle your nose, or open your eyes really wide and make the children curious about what you are doing. Let the children sit somewhere different, play the game in the housekeeping area or outside. The unexpected will prompt the curiosity of even the most distracted child.

Hello, bear!

Bring a new stuffed animal to a situation. Introduce the animal, choose a name together, and then give the stuffed animal to the most easily distracted child to hold carefully.

What's that?

Hide a book, picture, or object under a simple cloth on your lap. Add to the mystery by taking a peek; then, only when all the children are ready to pay attention, slowly remove the cloth.

Lost!

Rattle a bag of objects and pretend to have lost what you wanted to show the children. Pull out the objects one at a time!

Sit there!

Give each child a square of fabric to sit on. It defines her space and keeps her from invading other children's space.

Whisper!

Try whispering, singing very quietly, or using a silly voice to grab children's attention.

I can see you!

Cover your mouth with your hand and then, using a very obvious stare, move your head from side to side, looking at all the children one by one. When you have their attention, uncover your mouth and give them a big smile!

Smile!

And most important of all, smile! Give the children a great big welcoming smile. Be delighted that they have come to play, talk, or listen to you. Nobody wants to listen to someone who looks anxious, tired, bored, busy, or distracted. Give the children your full attention and they will give you theirs.

How to Use the Activities

This book offers a wide range of simple everyday activities and opportunities for counting. These will help you give young children the confidence to use their emerging counting skills and mathematical understanding at every opportunity.

Each activity page provides a list of what you need, as well as clear step-by-step instructions for the activity. A *look, listen, and note* list on each page gives pointers and tips on what to look and listen for, as well as things to think about as you play alongside and observe each child.

Each page also has additional activities to enable the child to practice the same skill and also ideas to take it further for children ready for more. When choosing extension activities, think about each child's learning style, his preferences and special interests, as well as how he makes sense of the world.

Page 75 has a list of counting action rhymes, songs, fingerplays, and stories that, together with the websites and resources mentioned in the activity pages, provide a wealth of additional material.

And, before you play the games and activities on the following pages, think about the kind of mathematical language that the children need to use and understand as they develop their counting skills.

Key words and phrases:
- All gone, more, again
- Same, different
- Few, many, lots, none
- One for you, one for me, share
- Zero, nothing
- Number, count
- Match, sort
- Order, first, last, second, third (and so on)
- Next, before, after
- Add, take away, total

Ideas to Share with Families

There is so much that families can do at home and when they are out and about to help their child with counting skills. Why not invite families to try out some of these ideas? Help the children make a poster of ideas for the families' information bulletin board. Here are some thoughts to get you started.

Families:
- Help your child share objects: "One for you, one for me," and so on.
- Practice matching one-to-one: one spoon in each cup.
- Find pairs together—pairs of the same object—such as socks or shoes, and pairs of objects that go together, such as cup and saucer, bowl and spoon.
- Count and sort laundry together as it comes out of the washing machine or is put out to dry.
- Count steps and stairs as you go up and down together.
- Count out food items as you shop: "Let's put three apples in here, one, two, three."
- Give your child a small bag or basket to fill with everyday items at home: "How many socks can fit in the basket? Can you find three toys?"

- Put some measuring spoons and cups in the sink with a little water and play at counting spoonfuls to fill cups.
- Share counting rhymes and books together.
- Try to use other mathematical language, such as "few," "lots," "more," "less," and "most."
- Look for opportunities to count when you are out and about. "How many cars are waiting at the traffic light? How many dogs can you see in the park?"
- At mealtimes, count the food items on each plate. Talk about how many you will have when you have eaten one. Don't forget zero or "all gone."
- Dressing and bath times are good times to count fingers and toes or play simple counting games.
- Listen to some nursery rhyme tapes together. Choose a favorite for your child to share with the other children at school or at home.
- Sing a simple commentary to describe your child's play as you watch or join in, such as "Thomas has three blocks" or "Look, this puzzle has 10 pieces."
- Blow some bubbles for your child. How many can she pop? Count together.

Counting Activities

Bowling Pin Splash

Focus: Guessing and rolling—a watery game for a warm day outside!

Vocabulary

another

different

empty

one more

pair

same

together

What you need

- at least five large, empty, clear plastic bottles (one-liter water bottles are ideal)
- box of balls of different sizes
- clean, non-slippery surface for children to move around barefooted
- warm day

What you do

❶ Help the children half fill the empty bottles with water and place them on a clean, flat surface outside.

❷ Take off shoes and socks!

❸ Take turns choosing a ball. Roll the balls one at a time at the row of water bottle "bowling pins."

❹ As soon as a bottle tips over, take turns rushing over and picking the bottle up again, saving as much water as possible.

❺ Guess the number of balls needed to empty the bottles.

❻ Count together. Talk about how much water is left in each "bowling pin."

Taking it further

- Label the bottles with numbers, using a marker. How many rolls are needed to knock over each numbered pin? Play again and aim to knock the balls over in numerical order.
- Add just a small amount of water to some bottles and fill others almost to the top. Play again, guessing how many balls it will take to knock over each bottle. Ask the children why they think some bottles are easier to knock over than others.

30 Fun Ways to Learn About Counting

shoes
& socks
removed

cement

Look, listen, and note

- Listen for the children counting spontaneously during the activity and commenting on how many more bottles they have to knock down.
- Watch to see if they can recall how many pins have been knocked down already.
- Listen for key words and ask open-ended questions to develop the children's confidence in predicting outcomes.

More ideas

- Add a few drops of food coloring to each bottle and seal tightly with the screw-top lids. Guess first, then count how many balls it takes to knock down each color.
- Stand an open, half-filled water bottle pin in front of each child. Take turns rolling the balls at each other's pins. Each child will need to jump out of the way when their pin tips over, and pick it up quickly to save any remaining water. Make it a really wet game, throwing soggy sponges at the pins! This idea is lots of fun outside on a hot day!

Ping-Pong Fun

Vocabulary

a few
all gone
high
less
lots
low
metal
more
noisy
on and under
silent

What you need

- low slide, or a slope created by placing a plank on a large block
- metal bucket or a large metal bowl
- 10 ping-pong balls

What you do

❶ Help the children collect the balls and then roll them down the slide into the bucket. Count them slowly. Talk about the wonderful sound the balls make as they drop into the bucket.

❷ Using the tune of "One, Two, Three, Four, Five, Once I Caught a Fish Alive," sing or chant:

One, two, three, four, five,   *Why did you let them go?*
Balls bouncing on the slide.   *Because they bounced so high and low.*
Six, seven, eight, nine, ten,   *One, two, three, four, five,*
Then we let them go again.   *Balls rolling down the slide."*

❸ Clap as you count and sing the song, then count the balls together as the children take turns releasing the balls down the slide.

Taking it further

- Help the children mark the balls with numbers. See if they can push them down the slide in order.
- Mark two balls with a number 1, two balls with number 2, and so on. Slide the balls down the slide, then challenge the children to find matching pairs.

low slide

ping-pong ball

metal bucket

Look, listen, and note

- Watch to see if the children can clap once for each count.
- Listen and note mathematical language used in context, such as "Look, two balls have rolled over there," and so on.
- See which children are able to take turns and join in confidently with this simple clapping game.

More ideas

- Try counting the balls as they drop onto a variety of surfaces. Encourage the children to guess what sounds they will make. Will they bounce high or low? Count the balls together as you test out their ideas.
- Roll the small ping-pong balls through a tube, counting as they go.
- Sit at opposite ends of a plastic or fabric play tunnel and sing, "One, two, three, go," before sending a large ball through the tunnel to a child at the other end. For older children, send armfuls of balls through at a time, counting together how many make it to the other end of the tunnel.

30 Fun Ways to Learn About Counting

Spotted Dogs

Focus: Counting and gluing fun with spots

Vocabulary

back
black
brown
ears
few
gray
hundreds
just one
lots
nose
paws
spotted
thousands
white

What you need

- collage materials, glue, or glue sticks
- images of Dalmatian dogs from magazines, catalogs, or the Internet
- plain paper and colored markers
- *Spot Can Count* by Eric Hill
- sticky label dots

What you do

❶ Look at the picture book together, counting as you go.

❷ Encourage the children to draw their very own spotted dog.

❸ Play alongside the children, encouraging them to draw and decorate their pictures with the spots and the other collage materials.

❹ Compare the children's pictures to pictures of Spot and other spotted dogs. Talk about the number and size of the spots. Try to count them together. Are there too many to count?

Taking it further

- Make 10 identical dog outlines and help the children create a spotted dog number line. The first dog will have one spot, the second will have two spots, and so on. Mark the numerals on the reverse side. Have fun putting the dogs in order, using first the spotted side and then the numerals.
- Take one of the dogs away. Can the children figure out which one is missing?

sticky label dots

Look, listen, and note

- Listen for the children relating what they are doing to stories from their own lives, about dogs or spotted patterns.
- See if the children are able to recall moments from the storybook while they are making their own pictures.
- Listen and note use of key words.

More ideas

- Spend time together in the book area finding all the counting picture books.
- Visit the library together and find *Ten Little Rubber Ducks* or *1, 2, 3, to the Zoo*. (These are counting books by Eric Carle that are great for counting together.)
- Display all the spotted dogs the children created on a spotted background, with a collection of the children's favorite counting books.

Beat that Drum

4

Focus: Counting to a steady beat

Vocabulary

first
listen
loud
quick
quiet
ready
slow
steady
together

What you need

● small drum and drumstick or can and wooden spoon
● some simple wooden blocks

What you do

❶ Practice counting together to a steady beat on the drum. Take turns making the beat.

❷ Working in pairs, build towers of five blocks each, counting and placing each block one at a time to the beat of the drum.

❸ As soon as the towers are built, bang the drum loudly and knock the towers down.

❹ Speed up the beat, and build and count the blocks quickly. Try it again really slowly.

Taking it further

● Chant: "Build a house with five blocks, 1, 2, 3, 4, 5," counting and building to the beat of the drum.

● March and count together, with each child taking turns leading with the drum.

● Play "One Potato, Two Potato, Three Potato, Four." Stack your hands one on top of the other, counting as you stack.

Look, listen, and note

● Watch to see if the children can match their counting to the beat.

● Listen to the way they use numbers and counting in their child-initiated free play.

- See how the children react when the beat changes. Can they adapt their counting to match the pace of the beat?

More ideas

- Use upturned empty yogurt containers for tiny finger drums. Take turns counting and hitting the drums with your fingers to the count of three. Try varying the rhythm and using a different singing voice to count.
- Place one, two, or three stickers on chime bars. Work together to arrange the chime bars in order of the number of spots. Count and play together.
- Play a simple hand-stacking game in pairs. Place one hand flat on the table, then the partner places her hand gently on top, and so on, counting to the steady beat of the drum.
- Put together a collection of different types of percussion instruments and experiment with counting and copying different rhythms and beats.

5 Ten Terrible Dinosaurs

Focus: A turn-taking guessing game

Vocabulary

few

fewer

guess

handful

less

lots

many

more

next

right

several

What you need

- 10 small dinosaurs
- box or cup big enough to hold all the dinosaurs
- *Ten Terrible Dinosaurs* by Paul Stickland

What you do

❶ Look at the book and count together.

❷ Sit together on the floor in a circle. Put the dinosaurs in the cup and pass the cup around the circle. Chant together, "10 terrible dinosaurs, one, two, three, four, ROAR!" After the roar, the child holding the cup should pour some dinosaurs into the next child's cupped hands.

❸ Ask that child to guess how many dinosaurs he is holding. Then ask him to toss the dinosaurs onto the floor in the middle of the circle.

❹ Count the dinosaurs together. Did the child guess more or less than the count?

❺ Continue playing until everyone has had a turn.

Taking it further

- Can the children guess how many dinosaurs are left in the cup? Count the dinosaurs on the floor together and then continue counting to 10 with the dinosaurs left in the cup.
- Line the dinosaurs up in pairs. Try counting from left to right, one to 10; then ask the children to find the first dinosaur, the fourth dinosaur, and so on.

30 Fun Ways to Learn About Counting

different color dinosaurs

Look, listen, and note

- Consider each child's understanding of numbers and quantity. See if the children are making realistic estimates.
- Listen for words that describe quantities, such as "lots," "many," and "several."
- Think about the children's memory skills. Can they recall how many dinosaurs other children had when it was their turn?

More ideas

- Dip the dinosaurs' feet in paint and try some printing and counting experiences together.
- Put the dinosaurs on the floor and cover with a large piece of netting or sheer fabric. Have the children take turns wriggling underneath to see how many dinosaurs they can find.
- Put some plastic containers and the dinosaurs in the sand tray. Hide all the dinosaurs in the plastic pots and then play a guessing-and-counting game to find how many dinosaurs are hiding in each place.
- Check out preschoolrainbow.org/preschool-rhymes.htm for great dinosaur-counting rhyme and dinosaur activities.

6 Big Box Guessing Game

Focus: Pushing, pulling, and counting using stuffed animals and big boxes!

Vocabulary

bigger
different
empty
full
heavy
less
light
more
same
smaller

What you need

- lots of teddy bears and stuffed animals
- marker
- several large cardboard boxes
- timer or simple clock

What you do

1. Sort the stuffed animals into groups of teddy bears, animals, dolls, and so on. Help the children count how many toys are in each pile.
2. Mark each box with the number of toys in the pile, such as 10 teddy bears, five dolls, and so on, using either a numeral or a matching number of dots.
3. Mix all the stuffed animals together.
4. Set the timer to one minute and challenge the children to sort all the toys and stuff them into the right boxes as fast as they can!
5. Count together how many toys are in each box, and check that this matches the mark on the box.

Taking it further

- Sort and count the toys according to different properties, such as 10 small stuffed animals in this box and 10 large toys in another, or perhaps all the puppets in here and all the dolls in here.
- Write a numeral on a sheet of paper and place it in each empty box. Challenge the children to fill all the boxes with the right number of toys, against the clock.

30 Fun Ways to Learn About Counting

timer

Look, listen, and note

- Watch to see how the children work together. Are they using mathematical language as they sort the toys?
- Listen for how they sort out issues, such as, "Look, we need three more in this box."
- Do the children retain their counting skills as they work under the pressure of the timer?

More ideas

Tip: Be sure you have cleared plenty of open space for these activities!

- Invite a child to hide in a box with 10 stuffed animals, too! Sing, "There were 10 in the bed and the little one said . . .," changing the words to: "There were 10 in the box and the big one said, "Out you go," throwing a toy out of the box one at a time, to fit the rhyme.
- Make a line of stuffed animals on the floor and make a parallel line with the boxes, 10 feet away. Play a racing game as children race from the boxes to the toys and back again, filling the boxes with the toys.
- All grab armfuls of stuffed animals and count down from 10 to one. On "one," toss the toys high in the air!

7 Pirates' Treasure

Focus: Sparkly one-to-one correspondence with a treasure theme

Vocabulary

complete

empty

few

full

less

lots

more

most

one

one at a time

row

same

What you need

- gold or silver cupcake liners
- *How I Became a Pirate* by Melinda Long, or another pirate picture book
- muffin or cupcake pans
- plastic coins, sequins, gems, and shiny buttons
- silver or gold spray paint (optional)

What you do

❶ If you want to spray paint the muffin pan, do so outside on a calm day, in a child-free zone. Take careful note of safety instructions on the paint can. Check that the muffin pans are completely dry before use.

❷ Read the story together.

❸ Mix the coins, sequins, gems, and buttons together.

❹ Play alongside the children, sorting and counting the pirates' treasure. Encourage the children to put one coin or gem in each cupcake liner, and place that in each compartment of the muffin pan. Count slowly together, matching one count for each piece of treasure placed.

Taking it further

- Write the numerals one to 10 on 10 cupcake liners. Help the children put these in numerical order and add the correct number of shiny sequins to each one.
- Add some tiny scoops or small spoons. Put one scoop of dry cereal in each cupcake liner. Help the children count the cereal as they eat it.

30 Fun Ways to Learn About Counting

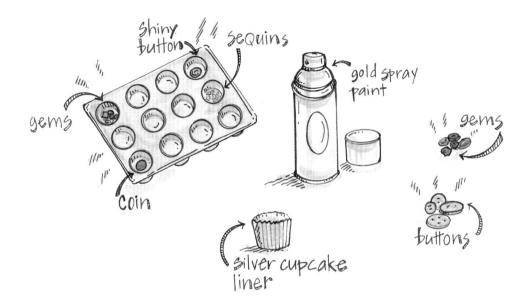

shiny button

sequins

gems

coin

gold spray paint

gems

buttons

silver cupcake liner

Look, listen, and note

- Watch to see if the children can match one count to each item they put in the containers.
- Pause suddenly and see if the children are able to continue counting unassisted.
- Listen to the language they use to share and compare their treasure.

More ideas

- Use tiny boxes to make treasure chests. See how many pieces of treasure will fit in each treasure chest.
- Make pretend treasure coins from aluminum foil and other shiny paper. Paint some treasure chest pictures and count the coins as you paste them in place.
- Find online counting games at familyfun.go.com/printables or other websites.
- Wrap pretend gems and other treasure in layers of tissue paper. Guess how many layers there are on each treasure package, and then count together as you unwrap the gems.

Hip Hop, Bunny Hop

Focus: Hopping, bouncing, and jumping as you count to three

Vocabulary

count

go

group

hop

one, two, three

ready

stop

together

wait

What you need

- lots of energy
- small bell or chime bar and a striker
- wide open space

What you do

❶ Help the children form groups of three.

❷ Ask the groups to arrange themselves so when the children spread their arms wide they cannot touch each other.

❸ Sound the bell or chime bar quietly and explain that this is the signal to stop and sit down. Practice this with the children!

❹ For this action rhyme, the children need to stay together in their groups of three.

❺ Sing or chant the following and lead the actions:

Hip hop, the bunny bop. (hands held as paws crouching down)
Hip hop, the bunny bop. (bouncing on the spot)
One, two, three, follow me. (slow bunny jumps, beckoning others to follow)

Jump little bunnies, jump, jump, jump. (slow deliberate big jumps)
Jump little bunnies, one, two, three. (quick tiny bunny jumps)
Jump little bunnies, follow me slow. (deliberate big jumps)

Hip hop, the bunny bop. (hands held as paws crouching down)
Hip hop, the bunny bop. (quick tiny bunny jumps)
One, two, three, follow me. (quick tiny bunny jumps)
Hip hop, STOP. (stop suddenly and sound the bell/chime bar)

30 Fun Ways to Learn About Counting

Group of three

hands
held as
paws

crouching
down

Taking it further

- Try more verses with the bunnies running, hopping (from one leg to another), or scampering on hands and feet.

Look, listen, and note

- Watch to see if the children can match their jumps and hops to the one, two, three count. Are they able to work cooperatively?
- See how quickly they can respond to the change of pace.
- Are the children able to anticipate the end of the rhyme? Do they make suggestions for more actions?

More ideas

- Give each group of three children a bucket and ask them to find one car, two books, three spoons, and so on.
- Make a big "One, Two, Three" book with illustrations from the children's favorite counting rhymes. Add simple text to support the children's pictures.

Traffic Jam

Focus: Counting to five and back again

Vocabulary

backward

countdown

fifth

first

forward

fourth

one way

reverse

road

second

third

What you need

- bikes, scooters, outdoor vehicles
- chalk
- five child-size traffic cones
- large outdoor play area
- roll of colored tape and scissors

What you do

❶ Mark out a wide road outside using the chalk. Make the road twist and turn. Mark it "ONE WAY" with a big arrow!

❷ Help the children put one band of tape around the first cone, two bands of tape around the second cone, and so on for all five traffic cones.

❸ Together, spread the cones out around the road.

❹ Bike, in convoy, from one cone to the next, in order, from one to five.

❺ Now ask the children to try it independently, calling out how many rings are on each cone as they go past.

❻ Try reversing from five down to one!

Taking it further

- Make flags together, decorated with one to five wheel prints, to add to each cone.
- Give each child a ticket with the numbers of the cones they should visit in order, such as three, two, one, or one, three, five.
- Make some simple cardboard traffic lights and other road signs to add.

30 Fun Ways to Learn About Counting

Look, listen, and note

- Watch and see if the children need to stop and count the rings on each cone or if they are able to say accurately at a glance how many rings are on the cone.
- Listen for the children who can confidently count from one to five and count down from five to one.
- Observe counting skills. Can the children maintain accurate counting when they are busy racing around the track?

More ideas

- Set up a train track and use colored sticky dots to label five tunnels, one to five. See if the children can take their trains through the tunnels in order from one to five and then back again from five to one.
- Make simple paper boats. Add spots to their sails. Blow them across the water tray. How many spots are on the winning sail?

10 Mini Mosaics

Focus: Shapes and counting using simple patterns

Vocabulary

big

bigger

biggest

billions

hundred

millions

mosaic

pattern

shape

size

small

smaller

smallest

square

thousands

tiny

What you need

- colorful pictures from magazines and junk mail
- glue or glue sticks
- hole punch
- pens and scissors
- plain paper

What you do

❶ Type the word "mosaics" into a search engine to look for images of mosaics. Print some pictures for inspiration and so children know what a mosaic is.

❷ Help the children draw some very simple shape outlines to make into mosaics—flowers, houses, vehicles, and so on.

❸ Cut and tear small shapes from the newsprint and magazine pages to make mosaic shapes.

❹ Use the hole punch to make little, round mosaic shapes.

❺ Talk to the children as they work, guessing and counting how many shapes will be needed to fill each part of their mosaic design.

❻ Work alongside the children, talking about their pictures and the Internet images. Use some big number words, such as "hundreds," "thousands," and "millions."

Taking it further

- Cut out lots of mosaic pieces in the shapes of circles, triangles, and squares. Count and sort the shapes as they are glued into place. Talk about and count the number of sides and corners on each shape.

- Introduce the idea of repeating patterns of colors or shapes into your work on the mosaics.

Look, listen, and note

- Watch to see if the children can keep the count going as they work, remembering how many pieces they have already placed. Or do they need to count from the beginning each time?
- Do the children know some very large number words, such as "millions"? Do they use these words appropriately in their play?
- Look to see if the children can cut and tear paper approximately to fit the space available on their designs.

More ideas

- Make some large mosaic shapes from cardboard boxes. Use these outside to fill chalk shapes on the ground.
- Smooth wet sand with a roller. Use a plastic block to make prints in the sand. Use the printing block to make mosaic-style pictures in the sand. Count together as the children print in the damp sand.

Kangaroos Against the Clock

Focus: Counting and one-to-one correspondence in an active game of collecting and jumping

Vocabulary

adult
baby
empty
few
full
joeys
kangaroo
less
lots
many
marsupial
more
none
pouch

What you need

- about 20 kangaroo images for every four children
- aprons with a pouch or large pocket at the front
- card stock
- egg timer, sand timer, or very simple clock
- glue
- safety scissors

A Little Tip

Use a search engine to find images of kangaroos, or print the kangaroo coloring page at: nationalgeographic.com/coloringbook/kangaroos.html.

What you do

❶ Look at the kangaroo images together. Talk about kangaroos carrying their very tiny babies in their pouches.

❷ Try out different ways that the kangaroos might move with their powerful hind legs and small raised forelegs. Try moving on all fours, tiny bounces upright and big, powerful bounds.

❸ Working together, cut out the kangaroo images and paste each one to a piece of card stock.

❹ Spread the images on the floor and give each child an apron to wear. Show the children how they can slip the kangaroo images into the pouch on the front of their aprons, just like mother kangaroos taking care of their joeys.

❺ Set the timer for one minute and ask the children to bounce along like kangaroos, gathering up the kangaroo images into their pouches. When the time is up, count together how many kangaroos are in each pouch.

30 Fun Ways to Learn About Counting

hop up

apron with pocket

picture pasted on posterboard

hop down

Taking it further

- Make larger and smaller kangaroo cards by enlarging and shrinking one of the kangaroo images on a copier. Play again, counting how many kangaroos are in each pouch and sorting and counting the images by size, such as three tiny kangaroos.
- Look for picture books featuring kangaroos, such as *Kangaroo's Cancan Café* by Julia Jarman or the *Blue Kangaroo* series by Emma Chichester Clark.

Look, listen, and note

- Watch to see if the children are counting one-to-one as they collect each kangaroo card from the floor.
- Are the children able to make comparisons, such as, "You have three more kangaroos than me"?
- Look to see how the children negotiate obstacles and other children as they pick up the pictures.

More ideas

- Use animal matching pair cards and encourage the children to collect matching pairs of animals in their pockets. Try counting the pairs of cards in twos.
- Together read *Does a Kangaroo Have a Mother, Too?* by Eric Carle. Then visit the Eric Carle official website at eric-carle.com for ideas and inspiring pictures.

30 Fun Ways to Learn About Counting

12 Knives, Forks, and Spoons

Focus: Counting, matching, and sorting with familiar objects

Vocabulary

cutlery

damp

drain

dry

few

less

lots

many

match

more

same

set

sort

wet

What you need

- cardboard box
- dish rack
- dish towels
- dishwashing bowls
- gentle dishwashing liquid
- paper napkins
- plastic cutlery sets and cutlery trays

What you do

1. Play alongside the children, washing and drying the cutlery. Count each type of cutlery and match and sort them into the trays.
2. Play games like, "Can You Find Me Two Spoons and Three Forks?" and so on.
3. See how many full sets of knives, forks, and spoons the children can find.
4. Put down a handful of forks on the table and ask the children to find the same number of knives.
5. Make a pretend dishwasher from a dish rack and a cardboard box.

Taking it further

- Help the children wrap the dry cutlery in paper napkins. Make bundles of spoons and forks wrapped together, knives and forks wrapped together, and

30 Fun Ways to Learn About Counting

Look, listen, and note

- Listen to see if the children can "count on." For example, if they have two dry spoons and then pull out a third from the water, do they need to start counting again, or can they count on to three?
- Can the children glance at a group of three items and know that there are three without counting?
- Listen for other mathematical language, such as *same*, *different*, *pair*, *more than*, *less than*, and so on.

More ideas

- Put three spoons, two forks, and one knife on the tray. Let the children look at the tray for a few minutes and then while they are not looking, remove one item. Can they guess what you took from the tray? Count together to check.
- Make placemats for the housekeeping area from a piece of card stock. Draw a simple place setting outline with a knife, fork, and spoon on each mat. Add the outlines of a plate and a glass. Laminate if you can.
- Try washing and drying lots of different kitchen utensils: spoons, spatulas, whisks, jugs, strainers, and so on. Sort and count them by function, such as draining or measuring.

30 Fun Ways to Learn About Counting

13

Gobble, Gobble, Munch, Crunch

Focus: A hungry caterpillar dice game

Vocabulary

butterfly
caterpillar
change
chrysalis
dice
food
fruit
leaves
less
more
next
vegetables

What you need

- at least 30 small circles of green paper or card stock, about $1\frac{1}{2}$ inches across (adjust according to the size of your group)
- black marker
- crayons, chalk, glue, and glue sticks
- die with dots on each side
- sheet of paper for each child
- *The Very Hungry Caterpillar* by Eric Carle

What you do

❶ Read *The Very Hungry Caterpillar* together, making plenty of time for counting and talking about how much food the caterpillar needs to grow. Look at the shape of the caterpillar and talk about how it is growing.

❷ Help each child draw a single long, wavy line horizontally across his paper from left to right.

❸ Take turns rolling the die. When a child rolls a three, he can paste three circles on his line as part of his own caterpillar.

❹ When he rolls a one, two, four, or five, he can add that many items of food to his picture with the crayons and say "four strawberries," and so on. If he rolls a six, he can add six legs to his growing caterpillar.

❺ When a child's caterpillar stretches all the way across the page, that child can use crayon to draw its face.

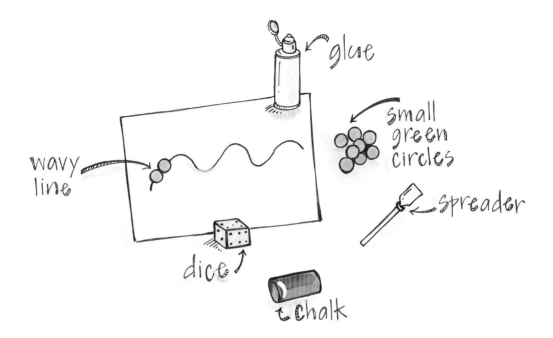

wavy line

glue

small green circles

spreader

dice

chalk

Taking it further

- Create beautiful butterfly pictures with wet chalk, or chalk on wet paper. Talk about the different patterns on butterfly wings.
- Go on a bug hunt, looking for and counting how many different insects you can find. Talk about how many legs each one has.

Look, listen, and note

- Observe the children's turn-taking skills. Can they maintain their attention when it is another child's turn?
- Watch and listen as the children count. Do they understand one-to-one correspondence?
- Listen to the kinds of language the children use to describe what they are drawing and how they relate this to everyday experiences.

Another idea

- Visit a traditional farmer's market or a grocery store. Spend time choosing and counting fruit and vegetables to make fresh juice or salad when you get back to school.

14

One, Two, Three, Four, Five

Vocabulary

catch
few
fit
float
large
lots
many
narrow
sink
small
wide

What you need

- blue and green food coloring
- red, yellow, or silver plastic folders (from dollar stores)
- scissors (for adult use only) and a permanent marker
- small plastic water bottles
- water table

What you do

❶ Cut small, simple fish shapes from the plastic folders. Make sure that the edges are smooth and safe for small fingers.

❷ Add a few drops of blue/green food coloring to the water table to make a warm, tropical ocean.

❸ Sprinkle in the fish. Count together how many float and how many sink.

❹ Use the small plastic bottles to catch the fish. Count together how many fish you catch in each bottle.

Taking it further

- Use colored cellophane and pieces of wool and ribbon to create seaweed. Add seashells and sand to create an ocean bed.
- Try catching the fish with strainers, colanders, or slotted spoons!
- Try to capture a specific number of fish in a bottle. Write a number on the outside of the bottle with a permanent marker. Go fishing, then count the fish together and talk about how many more are needed to fill each bottle.

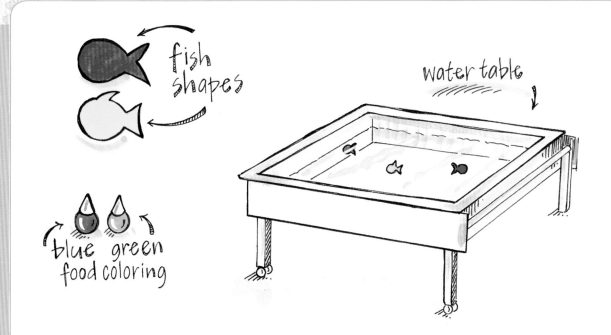

fish shapes

water table

blue green food coloring

Look, listen, and note

- Watch to see how the children work together. Are they able to comment on each other's successes?
- Listen for the children comparing the numbers of fish in each catch. What kind of mathematical language are they using?
- Do the children need to count aloud each time, or are they able to glance at the bottle and know instantly how many fish they have caught?

More ideas

- Read *The Rainbow Fish* by Marcus Pfister to the children.
- Glue strips of colored foil and paper to fish-shaped cards. Cover with tape or laminate to create larger individual colored fish or rainbow fish.
- Make some giant fish shapes out of newsprint. Lay these out on the floor and figure out how to blow or waft, for example, three shapes into one corner, or maybe two shapes over by the door, and so on.

Down the Drain

Focus: Counting backwards together

Vocabulary

again
center
down
edge
in
quickly
slow
sound
through
under
up

What you need

- large piece of fabric, perhaps an old curtain or sheet
- plastic bucket or crate
- scissors (for adult use only)
- small ball

What you do

❶ Spread out the fabric and have everyone sit on the floor, with the children arranged around the edges of the large cloth. Together, find the middle of the fabric and cut a hole the right size for the ball to slip through easily.

❷ Everyone stand up and hold onto the edges of the sheet, pulling it taut at the children's waist level. Place the bucket under the hole in the middle of the sheet.

❸ Place the ball on the sheet and count down together, "Five, four, three, two, one, IN!" Count together quickly or slowly, according to how long it is taking for the group to move the edges of the fabric up and down carefully to move the ball into the center and down the drain!

❹ Play again and again, seeing how quickly or slowly you can get the ball in the bucket, counting down each time.

Taking it further

- Play with two or three soft balls. Count down from 10.
- Play the game with lots of ping-pong balls. Count together how many you get in the bucket. Where are all the rest? Count them.

30 Fun Ways to Learn About Counting

- Hold the sheet taut and walk around in a circle. Sing or chant, "Round and round the garden like a teddy bear, one step, two steps, toss it in the air!" wafting the balls up and down gently on the fabric and at the end, throwing them high in the air!

Look, listen, and note

- Listen to how the children negotiate with each other and offer support.
- See if the children are able to count and concentrate on moving the ball around the fabric at the same time.
- Observe the children's problem-solving skills and listen to the language they use to comment on and question what is happening.

More ideas

- Share counting ideas with families. Look at www2.ed.gov/parents/ academic/help/math/part_pg5.html for lots of ideas.
- Use a long tube of cardboard (for example, from gift wrap) and a small ball or toy car. One child can hold the bucket and the rest can hold the tube. Push the ball or car down the tube and count down from five to one, while trying to get the ball or car to shoot out of the end of the tube into the bucket.
- Push lots of cars down the tube into the bucket, counting them as they land in the bucket.

16  Ten in the Bed

Focus: Simple pretend play and counting

Vocabulary

empty
few
first
last
left
less
lots
many
more
next
none

What you need

- 10 beanbags
- 10 teddy bears or other stuffed animals
- blanket

What you do

❶ Sing the familiar rhyme together, "There were 10 in the bed, and the little one said, 'Roll over! Roll over!' So they all rolled over, and one fell out. There were nine in the bed…."

❷ Count together as you place 10 teddy bears on the floor. Give each teddy bear a beanbag pillow, counting as you go.

❸ Take turns saying goodnight to each teddy bear, while the other children count as each bear goes to sleep!

❹ All together, cover the bears with the blanket.

❺ Sing the song together, taking one bear away at the end of each verse. Pause often to count how many bears are still in bed, how many pillows are empty, how many bears are awake, and so on.

Taking it further

- Play and sing again, taking two bears out at the end of each verse. "There were 10 in the bed, and the little one said, 'Roll over! Roll over!' So they all rolled over, and two fell out. There were eight in the bed… "
- Give each teddy bear a colored sticker. Play again, asking how many teddy bears with a red sticker are still in bed, and so on.

30 Fun Ways to Learn About Counting

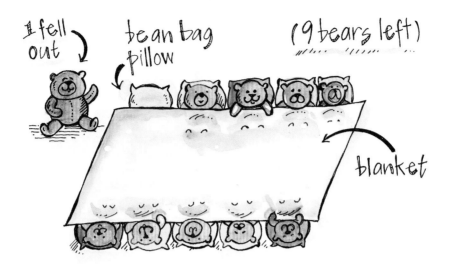

Look, listen, and note

- Notice what catches and holds the children's attention.
- Observe who has grasped the concept of one-to-one correspondence.
- Pause, and see if the children can continue counting independently.

More ideas

- Sing "Five Little Monkeys Jumping on the Bed."

  Five little monkeys jumping on the bed,
  One fell off and bumped his head.
  So Momma called the doctor, and the doctor said,
  "No more monkeys jumping on the bed!"
  Four little monkeys jumping on the bed…,
  Three little monkeys jumping on the bed…,

  Two little monkeys jumping on the bed…,
  One little monkey jumping on the bed…,
  No little monkeys jumping on the bed,
  None fell off and bumped his head.
  So Momma called the doctor, and the doctor said,
  "Put those monkeys back in bed!"

- Draw teddy bears, print free images of teddy bears from the Internet, or cut and tear teddy bear pictures from old magazines or catalogs. Work together to make a giant bear-shaped teddy bear collage using the small teddy bear images to fill in the bear shape. How many bears in total do you use?
- Make your own teddy bear pair matching game using a photocopier and the children's own drawings and other images.

Pasta Picnics

Focus: Counting spoonfuls and making shapes

Vocabulary

empty
few
full
heaping
level
lots
more
several
spoonful
words to describe
   the smell, color,
   and texture of
   ingredients

Think safety!

Check with families
for allergies and
special diets.

What you need

(adjust the quantities to the size of your group)
- ½ cup of small, cooked pasta shapes, rinsed
- bowls and spoons for each child
- chopped cucumber and avocado
- chopping boards
- plastic knives
- sharp knife (adult use only)
- small can of corn, opened and rinsed
- small container of natural yogurt
- two large tomatoes, washed and chopped
- vegetable peeler

What you do

❶ Start by washing hands together.

❷ Help each child put a mixture of pasta and corn into her bowl. Encourage the children to smell and taste the ingredients and to count out how many spoonfuls they use as they create their individual pasta salads.

❸ Let the children feel the unpeeled cucumber. Peel it and slice it in half lengthwise. Give each child a length of peeled cucumber and a spoon to scrape out the seeds. Help the children use plastic knives to cut their cucumbers into small pieces. Count the pieces.

❹ Add spoonfuls of chopped tomato and avocado to the salads.

❺ Taste, and then drizzle a spoonful of yogurt into each salad.

❻ At every stage, count spoonfuls of ingredients together. Talk about heaping and level spoonfuls.

30 Fun Ways to Learn About Counting

smelling

removing cucumber seeds

pasta

corn

yogurt

chopped tomatoes

avocado

Taking it further

- Gather together all the different sizes of spoons you can find in the classroom and arrange them together in size order, smallest to largest.

Look, listen, and note

- Observe the children's attention and listening skills. Are the children able to maintain their attention?
- Listen for the children to use language that compares quantities.
- Note the children's estimates of quantities in spoonfuls. Are they making realistic guesses?

More ideas

- Collect a range of different sizes of spoons, from tiny teaspoons to giant ladles. Add a range of different-sized plastic bottles and funnels. Make these available to the children to use as they play in sand or water. Count together how many spoonfuls are needed to fill the bottles.
- Use sets of measuring spoons, some flour, and small quantities of water for some very messy play; perhaps best outside!
- Tell the story of "Goldilocks and the Three Bears" and then make some porridge (or oatmeal) together using small, medium, and large spoons and bowls.

Bubble Fun

Focus: Have fun with this "Quick, Before it's Gone!" bubble game

Vocabulary

big

bubble

disappear

gone

huge

loop

mixture

pop!

small

soap

solution

sticky

What you need

- bubble mixture
- cotton string cut into about two-foot lengths, or bubble blowers
- large shallow tray
- sunny day—this is a game for outside

Tip

If you are making your own bubble mixture, add a few drops of glycerin (available from a drug store) to dishwashing soap and water.

What you do

❶ Tie the ends of each string together to form a loop.

❷ Dip the loops in the tray of bubble solution and blow gently. This is easier for some children than using bubble blowers.

❸ Count the bubbles together before they pop!

❹ Experiment with the bubble making. Does blowing hard make more bubbles? Can you make one huge bubble?

❺ Ask open-ended questions, but, equally important, share the children's joy and wonder at this simple activity.

Taking it further

- Try making lots of different bubble blowers using everyday objects, such as slotted spoons, plastic bowls, colanders, funnels, or the plastic loops that hold six-packs of cans together.

30 Fun Ways to Learn About Counting

- Gather together lots of junk plastic packaging. Dip this in the bubble solution and wave in the air. Guess which will create the most bubbles. Count the bubbles as they float away.

Look, listen, and note

- This is exciting play. Do the children retain their counting skills when they are excited and distracted?
- Listen to the language they use to describe, report, and predict what happens.
- Note the children's ability to estimate and compare quantities of bubbles.
- Look for developing eye-hand coordination.

More ideas

- Throw a handful of small craft feathers into the air. Count them quickly before they land!
- Dip a bouncy ball in water on a sunny day. Count the wet marks on the ground before they disappear.

Circle Time Treasure

Focus: How many altogether? Counting together as a group

Vocabulary

altogether

circle

coins

gems

jewels

pirate

sum

total

treasure

Tip

You will need enough "treasure" for each child to have at least three to four items, plus a few extra.

What you need

- basket
- box to use as a small treasure chest
- old necklaces, beads, bangles, and rings
- pretend coins—gold-painted cardboard circles
- pretend gems and jewels, made by gluing bright and shiny paper onto old CDs

What you do

❶ Sit in a circle on the floor and start circle or group time with the song "A Sailor Went to Sea" or your favorite ocean or pirate song.
Note: Use everythingpreschool.com/themes/ocean/songs.htm or another website to find a song.
A sailor went to sea, sea, sea,
To see what he could see, see, see.
But all that he could see, see, see,
Was the bottom of the deep blue sea, sea, sea!

❷ Next, place the treasure chest in the middle of the circle and all the jewelry, gems, and coins in the basket. Start the circle game by placing up to three items in the treasure chest and saying: "My name is sailor (name), and I am putting two rings and one coin in the treasure chest."

❸ Pass the basket to the first child in the circle so she can choose up to three items and repeat the phrase, "My name is sailor (name) and I am putting _____ in the treasure chest."

❹ Continue around the circle until everyone has had a turn.

5 Dump out the treasure and sort it: all the necklaces together, all the rings, all the coins or gems, and so on. Count how many are in each pile.

6 Next, put two piles together and count how many altogether.

7 Finish circle time by putting all the treasure back in the treasure chest and carefully passing the box around the circle as you repeat the opening song.

basket →

treasure chest

Taking it further

● Go around the circle asking the children to take turns putting, for example, three coins in the box, or four rings and one gem.

Look, listen, and note

● Consider the children's turn-taking skills and attention span. Can they remain focused on the activity when it is not their turn?

● Observe the way the children relate to each other. Are they anticipating their turn and what will happen next?

More ideas

● Design pirate flags together.

● Chalk a treasure map outline on the floor, or outside. Give the children chalk to add their own features to the map, such as mountains, rivers, and towns.

● Make 10 huge pretend coins by covering old CDs in colored foil. Hide these around the classroom and organize a treasure hunt. Stop after a few minutes and count how many have been found altogether.

● Bury lots of fake gems in wet sand in a shallow tray. At the end of play time, count how many have been discovered.

20 What's That?

Focus: More counting fun with very tiny objects

Vocabulary

big

bigger

fewest

hundreds

large

less

lots

magnify

many

millions

minute

more

most

small

thousands

tiny

What you need

- black paper
- plastic magnifying glasses
- scissors (for adult use only)
- silver ball cake decorations
- small bowls, one for each child
- tiny sequins
- tiny spoons or scoops

What you do

1. Prepare for this activity by cutting circles of black paper to line the insides of the bowls. This will provide a plain background.
2. Show the children the very tiny silver balls and sequins. Help them scoop just a few into each bowl.
3. Peer through the magnifying glasses and count the tiny decorations and sequins. Talk about which bowl has the most and which has the fewest of each kind.
4. Guess how many each bowl will have if you add another scoop to each. Add some more and count again.

Taking it further

- Take the magnifying glasses outside and see what other tiny objects you can find to count. Look at the undersides of leaves for bugs and eggs. Count petals, veins on leaves, the ridges in the bark of trees, and so on.

30 Fun Ways to Learn About Counting

silver ball cake decorations

black circle

- Back indoors, use the tiny spoons or scoops to sort the balls into one bowl and the sequins into another one. How many do you have in each bowl? How many altogether? Do you need the magnifying glasses to count them?

Look, listen, and note

- Watch the children as they scoop the tiny objects into their bowls. This requires considerable concentration and fine motor control. Note who is having difficulty and who gets frustrated easily.
- Listen to the children talk about their discoveries with the magnifying glasses. Do they show each other what they find?

More ideas

- With white glue and construction paper, make sparkly collages using the sequins and some glitter and the silver cake decorations. Once the glue is dry, you can experiment with looking at the artwork through the magnifying glasses.
- Encourage the children to look through the magnifying glasses at anything that interests them. What else can they find to count?

21

S-t-r-e-t-c-h!

Focus: Make some stretchy dough and practice counting as you s-t-r-e-t-c-h it.

Vocabulary

dough
flour
knead
length
measure
mixture
reach
smooth
sticky
stretch
thickness
water

What you need

- 1-cup measuring cup
- aprons
- bag of white flour
- large, flat surface
- rolling pins
- warm water to mix

What you do

1. Count out four cups of flour, putting them directly onto the table top. Feel the flour together. Wonder aloud how many grains of flour there might be in just one cup of flour. What is the biggest number the children can think of?

2. Sprinkle about a cup of warm water slowly onto the flour and gradually work it with your hands, bringing the flour and water together to make the dough. Add more flour or water to make a smooth dough that is not sticky.

3. Make a giant dough ball. Share it among the children and knead really well. The dough should be strong and smooth. The more you knead it, the stretchier it will be. If necessary, sprinkle the work surface with flour.

4. Bring all the dough together, knead again, and then use the rolling pins and hands to create a long sausage shape.

5. Now, with a child holding each end, lift the dough sausage up and swing it gently to and fro, stretching the dough. The dough will stretch quite some distance, maybe even across the room.

6. Put the dough sausage on the floor and ask the children to estimate how long the dough is. Count how many steps long the dough is. How many giant strides? How many tiny steps?

30 Fun Ways to Learn About Counting

4 cups of flour

warm water

giant dough ball

long sausage shape

Look, listen, and note

- Listen to the children's estimates of length. Do they show an understanding of how to measure length using numbers?
- Ask open-ended questions about the dough mixture and encourage the children to make comparisons with other textures and mixtures.

More ideas

- Glitter dough gives plenty of opportunity to talk about big numbers: hundreds, thousands, millions, and so on. Make glitter dough with three cups of plain flour, one cup of salt, one tablespoon of vegetable oil, one tablespoon of powder paint, water, and one tube of glitter. Mix all the dry ingredients together. Add the oil and water. Mix and knead well.
- Make soapy dough. Use two cups of flour, half a cup of salt, two tablespoons of powder paint, and one tablespoon of liquid soap in half a cup of water. Mix well.

Perfume Making

Focus: Deliciously smelly counting fun outside—a favorite of all children

22

Vocabulary

aroma
chop
grass
herb
leaf
perfume
petal
scent
slice
sliver
stem
texture
vein

What you need

- flower heads
- grasses
- herbs
- jug of water
- leaves
- plastic knives and small spoons
- small plastic bottles

What you do

❶ Take some time to examine the flowers. Look at and count the petals. Talk about the patterns and shapes you see. Explore the textures and scents of the flowers.

❷ Now examine the herbs. Talk about the shapes, aromas, and textures. Count the leaves and look at the way they are arranged on the stems.

FLOWERS

 rose

 mum

 violet

HERBS

 chives

 basil

 rosemary

30 Fun Ways to Learn About Counting

3 Pour a little water into each bottle and start to add petals and pieces of herbs to make "perfume."

4 Finely chop the herbs. Talk about the changing smells. Add some chopped herbs to the perfumes.

5 Continue to blend perfumes, counting how many leaves, petals, or blades of grass you add.

Taking it further

- Make labels for each perfume, adding a picture list of ingredients. Count the bottles. How many have, for example, yellow flowers?
- Take a walk together to gather more things to add to the mixture.
- Provide magnifiers to examine the ingredients.

Look, listen, and note

- Listen for the children counting confidently and independently. Are they using one-to-one correspondence?
- Listen for comparisons. Note the children finding similarities and differences.
- Think about the different ways the children are using mathematical language and counting skills to question, comment, and report what is happening.

More ideas

- Try mixtures on a grand scale. Gather leaves, mown grass, seeds, and soil, and stir with a large wooden spoon in a bucket. Make lots of opportunities for counting. Count each ingredient in handfuls.
- Make "magic potions" by adding spoonfuls of cooking oil to water. Try adding baking powder and just a teaspoon of vinegar (with close supervision). Once you add the vinegar, the mixture will bubble up and it may splash. Offer dried herbs, tea leaves, and spices for more potion-making.

23 Lemon and Lime Surprise

Focus: Floating, sinking, and counting with fruit

Vocabulary

bottom

experiment

float

heavy

large

lemon

light

lime

orange

peel

segment

sink

small

surface

top

What you need

- large and small oranges
- lemons in a bag
- limes (choose limes with thin skins)
- marker and paper
- water tray

What you do

❶ Wash all the fruit well in very hot water, or better still, choose unwaxed fruit.

❷ Make two columns on the paper; one with a picture of an object floating and one with a picture of an object sinking.

❸ Look at, feel, and count the lemons in the bag. Open the bag and feel the weight of a lemon. Do the children think it will float or sink?

❹ Ask each child to add a tally mark to the paper to record if he thinks it will float or sink. Count each column and then place the lemons in the water. Do they float or sink?

❺ Do the same with the limes and with the different-sized oranges. You may be surprised!

❻ Peel the fruits. Will they float or sink? Each time, record the children's predictions and count how many children think each item will float or sink.

Note: Use the lemons and limes to make lemonade or limeade for snack.

Taking it further

- Take digital photographs of each stage of the activity. Help the children put the photographs in order—"we did this first, second, third," and so on.

Look, listen, and note

- Listen to the children's use of language. Are they able to make comparisons and talk about their predictions?
- Watch as the children record their predictions. Are they able to say which number is greater and which is less? Discuss how many more children think an object will sink than think it will float, and so on.
- Observe the children's curiosity and wonder. Think about what is grabbing and holding their attention.

More ideas

- Make a collection of objects for more floating and sinking experiments. Try coins, keys, leaves, sponges, paper, empty plastic bottles with lids on, yogurt containers, and so on.
- Count a small handful of raisins into a small, plastic bottle of sparkling water or seltzer. Do they float or sink? Do the bubbles in the water make a difference? Try it with regular water.
- Try floating an egg in a bowl of water. Before you start, record how many children think it will float and how many think it will sink.

24  It's a Goal!

Focus: Fun with a lively soccer game of counting

Vocabulary

aim
goal
goalie
less
more
record
score
shoot
target
team

What you need

- chalk
- easel with a large sheet of paper
- soccer goal (or use two traffic cones)
- soft balls

What you do

1. If the goal is big enough, invite two children to be goalies together; otherwise play the game with one goal keeper.
2. Set up the easel next to the goal.
3. Line up the other children and agree on a target number of goals for the team, perhaps five to start with. Ask one of the children to draw five soccer balls on the paper at the easel. Count together to check the number.
4. Mark a spot for the ball in front of the goal. Take turns trying to score a goal. For each goal scored, the scorer needs to run up and cross out one of the balls drawn on the easel. Count again to see how many more goals are needed.
5. Continue with frequent counts until the target number of goals has been reached.
6. Play again with new goal keepers.

Taking it further

- Record the score with numerals as well as picture markers.
- If appropriate, add a challenge by using a timer. Count how many goals can be scored in two minutes.

- Change goal keepers every time a goal is scored. This makes maintaining concentration on the counting much more challenging.

Look, listen, and note

- Watch to see if the children are keeping score. Do they always know how many more goals they need?
- Listen to the way they encourage each other. Look to see if a leader is emerging.
- Think about how the team is working together. Do you think all the children are focused and part of the team?
- Note how the children negotiate the space and each other as they run around.

More ideas

- Set out a slalom course of cones for the children to dribble a soft soccer ball around. Ask them to count the cones as they pass them.
- Use masking tape to make numbers on the children's shirts to create your very own soccer team. Let each child choose her own number. With each choice, see if the group can jump that many times on the spot! Jump and count together.

30 Fun Ways to Learn About Counting

Tricky Triangles

25

Focus: Counting corners and sides

Vocabulary

corner

edge

mosaic

next

pattern

row

shape

side

triangle

What you need

- child-safe scissors
- corrugated cardboard
- different colors, textures, and weights of paper, including tracing paper and paper towels
- glue or glue sticks
- paper torn from magazines and newspapers
- printer paper
- thin foam (from a craft store)

What you do

1. Draw a large triangle shape on the printer paper. Make smaller triangle shapes to create a template for a triangle mosaic.

2. Work alongside the children, cutting and tearing triangle shapes from all the different colored paper and foam to create a giant triangle mosaic.

3. Glue the pieces onto a large piece of paper.

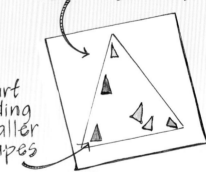

① triangle shape

② start adding smaller shapes

③ torn shapes

4 Count the corners and sides of each triangle as you glue it in place.

5 Sing the following to the tune of "Frère Jacques."

See my triangle, see my triangle.
Has three sides, has three sides.
Count them one, two, three.
Count them one, two, three.
Count with me, count with me.

6 Sing a second verse, counting corners instead of sides.

Taking it further

• Create a simple repeating pattern with color; first a red triangle, then a blue one, and so on.

• Provide some big triangles that cover several of the small triangles on the mosaic template.

• Use the triangles to create simple geometric pictures, such as a sailboat, a bridge, and so on.

Look, listen, and note

• Listen for the children counting spontaneously during the activity and naming the shape.

• Listen for the children working together and discussing the task.

More ideas

• Have a triangle tea party with triangle sandwiches, triangle-shaped carrot pieces, and triangle-shaped cookies.

• Make some triangle-shaped flags.

• Read *The Greedy Triangle* by Marilyn Burns about unusual places to find triangles.

26 Clip Art Crazy

Focus: Counting games using free clip art

Vocabulary

clip art
enlarge
fewest
image
large
most
picture
reach
reduce
small
stretch

What you need

- access to a photocopier or printer
- child-safe scissors
- clip art images
- paper bag and pen for each child
- scissors
- small mat or cushion for each child

What you do

❶ Print a page of clip art images from kidsturncentral.com/clipart or another source.

❷ With the children, make several copies of the page on the copier, enlarging some images and reducing the size of others.

❸ Count how many pages you have and count together how many images are on each page. Talk about enlarging and reducing the image on the copier. Find large and small copies of the same image.

❹ Cut the images out and gather them all into a pile.

❺ Ask each child to kneel on a cushion on the floor so he cannot reach any other child.

❻ Give each child a bag.

Print out

7 Sprinkle the images on the floor between the children. Now, say "Ready, Set, GO!" Ask the children to gather as many images as possible *without leaving their cushions.* They should put the images into their bags.

8 When all the images that can be reached are gathered into the bags, bring the children together and spend time counting together the pictures in each bag. Ask each child to mark his count on his bag.

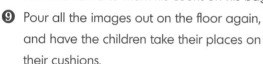

different size leaves

9 Pour all the images out on the floor again, and have the children take their places on their cushions.

10 Repeat the activity. When you count this time, did you have more pictures in your bag than you did the first time, or fewer?

Taking it further

- You can do this activity racing the clock. Set a timer for 30 seconds, and see how many pictures you collect. Try one minute.
- More clip art at: classroomclipart.com or from Dorling Kindersley at dorlingkindersley-uk.co.uk.

Look, listen, and note

- Observe the way the children maintain their balance, kneeling on the cushions while stretching to reach the pictures.
- Listen to their counting skills. Are they counting confidently and accurately?
- Are the children able to compare numbers? How do they record their counts on their bags?

More ideas

- Use the clip art images to make a matching pairs memory game.
- Hide the images around the classroom and challenge the children to find 10 each. Count often to see how many they have found. Ask how many they will have if they find one more.
- Put all the pictures on a small table. Each child asks a "storekeeper" for three dogs, two cars, and so on.

30 Fun Ways to Learn About Counting

27 Count Those Spots

Focus: Ladybug fun—a table-top counting race

Vocabulary

ahead

behind

first

in front

ladybug

second

space

third

track

What you need

- black pen
- die with spots
- ruler
- 6 ladybug shapes, about 4 inches long, cut from red paper
- 6 strips of green paper, each one approximately $3\frac{1}{2}$ feet long
- tape

What you do

❶ Draw lines at four-inch intervals across each of the strips of green paper.

❷ Tape the six strips of green paper to the table, parallel to each other, to create the lanes of a race track.

❸ Select six children and give each one a ladybug. Draw one spot on the first ladybug, two on the second, and so on. Place each ladybug at the beginning of the track.

❹ Take turns rolling the die. If a six is rolled, move the ladybug with six on its back along the track one space. If a five is rolled, move the ladybug with five on its back up the track one space, and so on. Who will reach the end of the track first?

❺ As you play, talk to the children about how many more spaces each ladybug needs to move. Ask which ladybug is ahead. How many spaces ahead are they?

❻ Repeat until each child who wants to has had a turn to race a ladybug.

30 Fun Ways to Learn About Counting

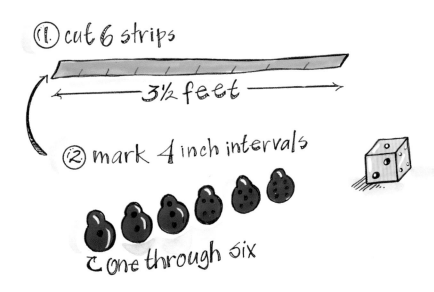

① cut 6 strips

← 3½ feet →

② mark 4 inch intervals

⎰ one through six

Taking it further

- Give each of the children a tiny piece of paper before each race and ask them to put the same number of spots on the paper as the ladybug they think will be the first across the finish line. Hide the papers until the end, then count the spots and compare.
- Put two ladybugs together and ask the children how many spots there are total.

Look, listen, and note

- Observe the children's matching and counting skills. Are they confident and secure in their knowledge?
- Can the children remain focused throughout the game?

More ideas

- For free ladybug activities, look at webtech.kennesaw.edu/jcheek3/ladybugs.htm.
- Read for *Are You a Ladybug?* by Judy Allen or *The Very Lazy Ladybug* by Isobel Finn.
- Use chalk to create huge ladybug shapes on the ground outside. Add a different number of spots to each ladybug. Play a listening game, asking the children to jump six times on the ladybug with six spots, clap three times on the ladybug with three spots, and so on.

28 Firefighters and Ladders

Focus: Up and down ladders to practice counting

Vocabulary

close

distance

far

ladder

less

more

near

rung

space

target

What you need

- chalk
- small buckets of water
- sponges
- sunny day

What you do

❶ Use chalk to draw a long ladder on the ground. Make the spaces between the rungs big enough for the children to jump in.

❷ Stand at the first rung and jump along the ladder in the spaces, counting as you jump from one space to the next. As you get to the end, the first child follows. All count together. Then the next child takes a turn. Continue until everyone has jumped up the ladder.

❸ Use red and orange chalk to draw a small fire in one of the spaces part-way up the ladder. Tell the children that they can use the sponges to put out the fire.

❹ Take turns throwing a sponge dipped in a bucket of water at the fire. Throw the sponges along the ladder from the first space. Count how many spaces the sponge has been thrown. How many more spaces did it need to go? Practice counting forward.

Taking it further

- Create two fire patches. Talk about how many spaces there are between the two fires. How many spaces to the first fire? How many to the second fire?

30 Fun Ways to Learn About Counting

sponge

chalk ladder

chalk fire

Small bucket of water

- Draw a new ladder. Ask the children how many more rungs they want to add to the ladder. Ask how many rungs the ladder will have if you add just one more rung, and so on.

Look, listen, and note

- Observe the accuracy of the counting. Are the children using one-to-one correspondence?
- Listen to the way the children share their ideas and problem solve, independently and together.

More ideas

- Check out the counting games, songs, and activities on the PBS website pbskids.org/games/numbers.html.
- Tape a large sheet of paper to a wall. Print a wall of blocks on the paper using plastic blocks dipped in paint. Count how many blocks are in each line. How many blocks are there in total? Carefully tear off a line of blocks. Ask how many lines are left.

Hoops and Loops

Focus: Beach ball croquet!

Vocabulary

arch
bat
croquet
first
least
less
more
most
second
third

What you need

- 10 cardboard boxes
- cardboard tubes from paper towel rolls
- marker
- sharp scissors (for adult use only)
- soft balls or inflatable beach balls

What you do

❶ Prepare for the activity by cutting deep arches in both sides of each cardboard box so when the box is upside down, the ball will fit easily through the box.

❷ Arrange the upside-down boxes around the floor.

❸ Take turns drawing one, two, or three smiley faces on the top of each box.

❹ Use the tube bats to gently tap the balls through each of the boxes with each child, counting how many smiley faces are on all the boxes their ball passes through.

Taking it further

- Record the number of smiley faces that each child counts on paper. Ask each child to draw that number of smiley faces next to her name. Count the smiley faces together. Every child should have the same number of smiley faces by the end.
- Give half the smiley faces hats! Play again, counting how many smiley faces with hats the children count as they tap their balls under the boxes.

Look, listen, and note

- Listen for number order words "first," "second," and so on.
- Watch to see if the children can "count on" from each box to the next. They are aiming to count the number of faces in total.
- Observe the children comparing totals.

More ideas

- Have the children keep track of how many taps it takes to get the ball through each box. Is it easier if the box is smaller? What if we use smaller balls?
- Make some simple smiley face stickers with blank labels and pens. Put up to five stickers on the back of a child's shirt. Can she guess how many faces are on her back? Give her clues of "more" or "less," and so on.

30 Finger Fun

Focus: Fingers are always best for counting!

Vocabulary

few

fingers

fingertips

greatest

index finger

knuckles

least

less

many

more

palms

thumb

What you need

- pieces of aluminum foil
- pieces of ribbon
- tape
- tiny sticky label dots

What you do

❶ Sit in a circle with the children. Sing the "You put one finger in" verse of "The Hokey Pokey."

❷ Try a few more verses and then ask the children to put tiny spots on some fingertips, put pieces of ribbon attached with tiny pieces of tape to other fingers, and wrap some fingers in aluminum foil. This is a great opportunity for the children to help each other.

❸ Sing the song again, this time, "You put your spotted fingers in. . .," or "You put your shiny fingers in. . .," or "You put your ribbons in. . . ."

❹ At the end of each verse, count together how many spotted fingers there are, how many ribboned fingers there are, and how many shiny fingers there are.

❺ Why not try it with toes?

Taking it further

- Hold up all fingers and take guesses on how many shiny fingertips there are, and so on. Count and compare the totals with the estimates.

ribbon with tape

shiny finger

Look, listen, and note

- Watch the way the children decide how to decorate their fingertips. Look for examples of kindness, helping, and cooperative play to praise.
- Listen to the language used to compare numbers.
- Use a sing-song voice for the counting. Vary this by singing in a whisper and then in a very deep voice, and so on. What grabs and keeps the children's attention?

More ideas

- Make lots of loose rings for little fingers with narrow strips of paper taped together with narrow tape. Decorate the paper with colored markers before taping into place.
- For lots of fingerplay ideas, try *The Complete Book of Rhymes, Songs, Fingerplays, and Chants* by Jackie Silberg and Pam Schiller.
- Try *Island Counting, 1, 2, 3* by Frané Lessac.
- Visit mother goose online (mothergoose.com/games/fingerplay) for a comprehensive listing of counting finger rhymes.

Index

A

Action rhymes, 73, 75
    "Hip Hop, the Bunny Hop," 28
Action songs, 8
Adapting, 21
Adding, 7, 11, 69
    songs, 75
    vocabulary, 9
Alike/different, 7, 11
Aluminum foil, 27, 72
Animals
    dinosaurs, 22–23
    fish, 40–41
    kangaroos, 34–35
    matching pair cards, 35
    stuffed, 10, 24, 44
Anticipating, 29, 51
Aprons, 34, 54
Art activities, 18–19, 32–33, 38, 39, 53
Attention-getting, 9–10, 45, 47, 51, 53, 59, 67, 73
Avocados, 46

B

Bags, 10–11, 58
    paper, 64
Baking powder, 57
Balance, 65
Balls, 14, 42–43, 49, 60, 70
    beach, 70
    ping-pong, 16, 42
    soccer, 61
Bangles, 50

Baskets, 11, 50
Bath time, 12
Beach balls, 70
Beads, 50
Beanbags, 44
Bells, 28
Bikes, 30
Blankets, 44
Blocks, 16
    plastic, 33, 69
Body parts, 8
Books, 10, 12, 19, 29
    1, 2, 3 to the Zoo by Eric Carle, 19
    Are You a Ladybug? by Judy Allen, 67
    Blue Kangaroo series by Emma Chichester Clark, 35
    The Complete Book of Rhymes, Songs, Fingerplays, and Chants by Jackie Silberg & Pam Schiller, 73
    Does a Kangaroo Have a Mother, Too? by Eric Carle, 35
    The Greedy Triangle by Marilyn Burns, 63
    How I Became a Pirate by Melinda Long, 26
    Island Counting, 1, 2, 3 by Frané Lessac, 73
    Kangaroo's Cancan Café by Julia Jarman, 35
    The Rainbow Fish by Marcus Pfister, 41
    Spot Can Count by Eric Hill, 18
    Ten Little Rubber Ducks by Eric Carle, 19
    Ten Terrible Dinosaurs by Paul Stickland, 22
    The Very Hungry Caterpillar by Eric Carle, 38–39
    The Very Lazy Ladybug by Isobel Finn, 67

Bottles, 14, 40, 47, 56, 59
Bowls, 46–47, 52, 59
    dishwashing, 36
    metal, 16
    plastic, 48
Boxes, 22, 24, 27, 33, 36, 50, 70
Bubble blowers, 48
Bubbles, 12, 48
Buckets, 29, 42–43, 57, 68
    metal, 16
Bulletin boards, 11
Butterflies, 39
Buttons, 8, 26

C
Cake decorations, 52–53
Calculating, 7, 9
Cameras, 58
Cans, 20
Card stock, 34, 38
Cardboard
    corrugated, 62
    tubes, 43, 70
Carrots, 63
Cars, 43
Catalogs, 18, 45
CDs, 50–51
Cellophane, 40
Cereal, 26
Chalk, 30, 33, 38–39, 51, 60, 67–68
Chalkboards, 8
Chants
    Building a House, 20
    One, Two, Three, Four, Five, 16
    Round and Round the Garden, 43
    Ten Terrible Dinosaurs, 22
Chime bars, 21, 28
Chopping boards, 46

Circle time, 50–51
Clapping, 16–17, 67
Clip art, 64–65
Clipboards, 8
Clocks, 24, 34, 65
Coins, 59
    cardboard, 50
    plastic, 26
Colanders, 40, 48
Collage materials, 18
Collages, 53
Colored foil, 41, 51
Colored stickers, 44
Colored tape, 30
Comparing, 7, 18, 35, 41, 55, 57, 59, 65, 71, 73
Concentration, 61
Construction paper, 53
Cookies, 63
Cooking oil, 55, 57
Cooperation, 21, 24–25, 28–29, 42–43, 60–63, 69, 72–73
Corn, 46
Corrugated cardboard, 62
Cotton string, 48
Counters, 8
Counting, 16–17, 20–21, 24–26, 30–47, 50–69, 72–73
    backward, 8, 25, 30–31, 42–45
    in everyday life, 7–12
    songs, 8, 11
    together, 48–49
"Counting on," 25, 37, 45, 71
Counting rhymes, 8, 11–12, 29
    Five Little Monkeys, 45
    Ten in the Bed, 44–45
Craft feathers, 49
Crates, 42

Crayons, 38
Cucumbers, 46
Cupcake liners, 26
Cupcake pans, 26
Cups, 22
    measuring, 12, 54–55
Curtains, 42
Cushions, 64
Cutlery trays, 36

D
Descriptive language, 34–35, 47, 49, 53, 59, 69, 73
Die, 38, 66
Dinosaurs, 22–23
Dish racks, 36
Dish towels, 36
Dishwashing bowls, 36
Dishwashing liquid, 36, 48
Dolls, 24
Drawing, 8, 18, 39
Dressing games, 12
Drums, 20
Drumsticks, 20

E
Easels, 60
Egg timers, 34
Eggs, 59
Environmental sounds, 8
Estimating, 7, 22–23, 47, 49, 54–55
Extension activities, 11
Eye-hand coordination, 14–17, 40–41, 48–49, 60, 68, 70

F
Fabric, 10, 23, 42
Families, 11–12, 43
Field trips

farmer's market, 39
grocery store, 39
Fine motor skills, 18, 26, 32–33, 38–39, 46, 52–53, 72
Fingerplays, 11, 73
Fish, 40–41
Fish-shaped cards, 41
Flags, 30, 51, 63
Flip charts, 8
Floating/sinking, 58–59
Flour, 47, 54–55
Flowers, 52, 56
Foam, 62
Foil
    aluminum, 27, 72
    colored, 41, 51
Food allergies, 46
Food coloring, 15, 40
Free play, 20
Fruits, 39, 58–59
    lemons, 58
    limes, 58
    oranges, 58
    raisins, 59
    tomatoes, 46
Frustration, 53
Funnels, 47–48

G
Games
    All Gone, 7
    Count Those Spots, 66
    Firefighters and Ladders, 68–69
    Gobble, Gobble, Munch, Crunch, 38–39
    Hoops and Loops, 70–71
    Kangaroos Against the Clock, 34–35
    One Potato, Two Potato, Three Potato, Four, 20

Soccer, 60–61
   Traffic Jam, 30–31
Gems, 26–27, 50–51
Geometric pictures, 63
Glitter, 53
Glitter dough, 55
Gloves, 8
Glue, 18, 32, 34, 38, 41, 53, 62
   sticks, 18, 32, 38, 62
Glycerin, 48
Grass, 56–57
Gross motor skills, 14–17, 24–25, 28–29, 34–35, 54, 60–61, 64–65, 67–69
Guessing, 7, 14–15, 17, 22–23, 27, 32, 49, 52, 71–72

H
Hand tally counters, 8
Herbs, 56–57
Hole punches, 32
Housekeeping corner, 37

I
Infants, 7
Insects, 38–39, 66–67
Internet, 18, 45

J
Jewelry, 50
Jewels, 50
Jugs, 37, 56
Juice, 39
Junk mail, 32
Junk packaging, 49

K
Kangaroos, 34–35
Keys, 59
Kindness, 73
Kitchen utensils, 37

Knives, 46
   plastic, 36–37, 46, 56

L
Labels, 9, 14, 57, 71
Ladles, 47
Ladybugs, 66–67
Laminate, 37, 41
Leadership skills, 61
Learning styles, 11
Leaves, 52, 56–57, 59
Lemonade, 58
Lemons, 58
Libraries, 19
Limeade, 58
Limes, 58
Line drawings, 8
Liquid soap, 55
Listening, 9, 67

M
Magazines, 18, 32, 45, 62
Magnifying glasses, 52–53, 57
Maps, 51
Marching, 20
Markers, 14, 18, 24, 38, 58, 70, 73
   permanent, 40
Masking tape, 61
Matching, 7, 11, 16, 20, 29, 35–37, 45, 65–67
Mathematical ideas, 9
Mathematical language, 7, 9, 12, 17, 22, 25, 27, 37, 39, 41, 43, 47, 57, 71
   key phrases, 11
Mathematical methods, 9
Mats, 64
Measuring, 8–9, 54–55
Measuring cups, 12, 54–55
Measuring spoons, 12, 47, 55, 57
Memory skills, 18, 23, 33, 37, 65

Mosaics, 32–33, 62–63
Moving/stationary objects, 8
Muffin pans, 26

N
Napkins, 36
Necklaces, 50
Negotiating, 35, 43, 61
Netting, 23
Newspaper, 62
Newsprint, 41
Number cards, 8
Number concepts, 7, 23
Number labels, 8
Number recognition, 9, 18, 24, 26, 30, 40, 60
Number words, 7, 9, 22–23, 32–33, 55, 71, 73
Nursery rhymes, 12

O
Oatmeal, 47
One-to-one correspondence, 7, 11, 24, 26–27,
        35, 39–40, 45, 57, 69
Open-ended questions, 15, 48, 55
Oranges, 58
Ordering, 11, 14, 16, 18, 21, 26, 31, 47, 58
Outdoor activities, 14–15, 28–31, 33, 39, 47–49,
        51–52, 56–57, 67–69
Outdoor vehicles, 30

P
Paint, 23, 27, 69
    powdered, 55
    spray, 26
Pairs, 7, 11, 16, 22, 35
Paper, 18, 24, 32, 38–39, 41, 52, 58–60, 62, 66,
        69–70, 73
    card stock, 34, 38
    construction, 53
    newsprint, 41

printer, 62
shiny, 27, 50
tissue, 27
tracing, 62
Paper bags, 64
Paper boats, 31
Paper napkins, 36
Paper towels, 62
    tubes, 70
Pasta shapes, 46
Patterns, 7, 9, 33, 63
Pens, 32, 64, 66, 71
Perfume making, 56–57
Permanence, 8
Permanent markers, 40
Photocopiers, 35, 45, 64
Pictures, 8, 10, 32
    Dalmatians, 18
    kangaroos, 34–35
    mosaics, 32
    teddy bears, 44–45
Ping-pong balls, 16, 42
Pirates, 26–27, 50–51
Placemats, 37
Planks, 16
Planning, 7
Plastic blocks, 33, 69
Plastic bottles, 14, 40, 47, 56, 59
Plastic bowls, 48
Plastic coins, 26
Plastic containers, 23
Plastic folders, 40
Plastic knives, 36, 46, 56
Plastic pots, 23
Plastic six-pack rings, 48
Play tunnels, 17
Porridge, 47
Posters, 11

Predicting, 7, 14–15, 49, 58–59, 67

Pretend play, 44–45

Printer paper, 62

Printers, 64

Problem solving, 7, 9, 43, 69

Puppets, 24

R

Raisins, 59

Recall, 15, 19

Resources, 11

Rhythm, 20–21

Rhythm instruments, 20–21

Ribbon, 40, 72

Rings, 50, 73

Rollers, 33

Rolling pins, 54

Rulers, 66

S

Salads, 39

Salt, 55

Sand, 33, 40, 47, 51

Sand timers, 34

Sand trays, 23

Sandwiches, 63

Scissor skills, 32–33

Scissors, 30, 32–34, 40, 42, 52, 62, 64, 70

Scoops, 26, 52

Scooters, 30

Seashells, 40

Seeds, 57

Self-confidence, 7, 10, 15, 17, 31, 57, 65, 67

Seltzer, 59

Sequencing, 7, 11

Sequins, 26, 52–53

Shapes, 32–33, 46–47, 62–63

Sharing, 7, 11

Sheets, 42

Shoes, 8

Singing, 10

Sinks, 12

Size, 24, 35, 47, 64

Slalom courses, 61

Slides, 16

Slotted spoons, 40, 48

Smiling, 10

Snacks

    lemonade, 58

    limeade, 58

    oatmeal, 47

    pasta salad, 46

    porridge, 47

    triangle tea party, 63

Soapy dough, 55

Soccer balls, 61

Soccer goals, 60

Socks, 8

Soil, 57

Songs, 11

    "Five Little Monkeys Jumping on the Bed," 45

    "One, Two, Three, Four, Five," 16

    "Round and Round the Garden," 43

    "A Sailor Went to Sea," 50

    "See My Triangle," 63

    "Ten in the Bed," 25, 44–45

    "You Put One Finger In," 72

Sorting, 7–8, 11, 24–26, 32, 35–37, 51, 53

Space, 9

Sparkling water, 59

Spatulas, 37

Spices, 57

Sponges, 15, 59, 68

Spoons, 26, 37, 46–47, 52, 56

    ladles, 47

    measuring, 12, 47, 55, 57

    slotted, 40, 48

wooden, 20, 57
Spray paint, 26
Stickers, 21, 71
   colored, 44
Sticky label dots, 18, 31, 72
Stories, 11
   "Goldilocks and the Three Bears," 47
Strainers, 37, 40
Stretchy dough, 54–55
Strikers, 28
String, 48
Stuffed animals, 10, 24, 44
Subtracting, 7, 11, 44–45, 69
   songs, 75
   vocabulary, 9
Symbolic representation, 8

T
Tables, 21, 65
   water, 40
Taking turns, 14–17, 20, 22–23, 39, 51, 66, 68
Tallying, 8
Tape, 41, 66, 72–73
   colored, 30
   masking, 61
Tea leaves, 57
Team work, 61, 63, 69
Teddy bears, 24, 44
Tickets, 30
Timers, 24, 34, 60, 65
Tissue paper, 27
Tomatoes, 46
Tracing paper, 62
Traffic cones, 30, 60–61
Traffic lights, 30
Train tracks, 31
Transience, 8

Trays, 37, 48, 51
   cutlery, 36
   sand, 23
   water, 31, 58
Tubes, 17
   cardboard, 43, 70

V
Vegetable oil, 55
Vegetable peelers, 46
Vegetables, 39
   avocados, 46
   carrots, 63
   corn, 46
   cucumbers, 46
Vinegar, 57
Vocabulary, 7, 9, 11–12, 17, 23, 25, 27, 32–33, 37, 39, 41, 43, 47, 55, 57, 71, 73

W
Water, 12, 33, 39–40, 47–49, 51, 54–57, 68
   sparkling, 59
Water tables, 40
Water trays, 31, 58
Websites, 11, 23, 27, 34–35, 43, 50, 64–65, 67, 69, 73
Weight, 58
Whisks, 37
Whispering, 10
White boards, 8
Wool pieces, 40
Wooden spoons, 20, 57
Wrapping paper tubes, 43

Y
Yogurt, 46
   containers, 21, 59

Z
Zero, 7, 11, 12

30 Fun Ways to Learn About Counting